First Ladies

Martha Washington

Joanne Mattern

ABDO
Publishing Company

visit us at
www.abdopublishing.com

Published by ABDO Publishing Company, 8000 West 78th Street, Edina, Minnesota 55439.

Printed in the United States.

Cover Photo: Getty Images
Interior Photos: Alamy p. 21; AP Images pp. 23, 25; Corbis pp. 5, 16, 22, 27; Getty Images pp. 19,
    31; Library of Congress pp. 8, 11, 13, 15, 17, 24; North Wind pp. 7, 12, 14, 18, 20, 26;
    Washington-Custis-Lee Collection, Washington and Lee University, Lexington, Virginia pp. 9, 10

Series Coordinator: BreAnn Rumsch
Editors: Rochelle Baltzer, BreAnn Rumsch
Art Direction & Cover Design: Neil Klinepier

Library of Congress Cataloging-in-Publication Data

Mattern, Joanne, 1963-
  Martha Washington / Joanne Mattern.
      p. cm. -- (First ladies)
  Includes index.
  ISBN 978-1-59928-801-7
  1. Washington, Martha, 1731-1802--Juvenile literature. 2. Presidents' spouses--United States--
Biography--Juvenile literature. I. Title.

  E312.19.W34M38 2008
  973.4'1092--dc22
  [B]   450 286 5

                                                                                    2007009761

Contents

Martha Washington

Martha Washington was the first woman to become First Lady of the United States. Her husband George Washington was the country's first president. Together, they led the nation from 1789 to 1797.

President Washington faced many challenges as the leader of a new nation. And, there was no one to show him what to do! No one had ever been First Lady before either. Sometimes, Mrs. Washington did not enjoy this job. But, she always did her best to help the president through difficult times.

Many women looked up to Mrs. Washington. She worked hard to be a leader. Mrs. Washington wanted everyone to know that the United States was an important country. Family life was also special to her. These qualities made her a positive role model for Americans. Through her actions, Mrs. Washington set the standard for the role of First Lady.

Martha Washington was hesitant to act as an official First Lady. However, her courage laid the foundation for the many First Ladies who have followed.

Plantation Life

Martha Dandridge was born on June 2, 1731. She was the oldest of eight children. Martha was called Patsy when she was a little girl. She and her family lived on a plantation near Williamsburg, Virginia. At the time, Virginia was a colony of Great Britain.

Martha's parents were John and Frances Dandridge. John was a tobacco farmer. The Dandridge family lived comfortably in a beautiful house called Chestnut Grove. Like other plantation families, the Dandridges had slaves. Their slaves cooked and cleaned in the house and picked tobacco in the fields.

Martha and her sisters spent their days learning how to be good wives and mothers. Frances taught the girls many things. They grew and harvested their food by hand. Martha learned to sew and cook. She also learned how to run a house and care for children.

In colonial times, most girls did not attend school. However, Martha was lucky. Her mother taught her how to read, write, and do mathematics.

During the 1700s, caring for the household took all day! So, children were expected to help with many chores.

First Love

During colonial times, women learned many other important skills. Martha learned to ride a horse. She could also play the piano and sing. And, she knew how to dance and host parties. When Martha turned 15, she began attending social events.

Martha and her parents sometimes went to Williamsburg, where they attended fancy parties. At one such party, Martha met Daniel Parke Custis. He was 20 years older than Martha. Daniel was a kind, wealthy man. He owned a large plantation near Chestnut Grove.

Martha and Daniel liked each other right away. So on May 15, 1750, they were married

At first, Daniel's father did not approve of Martha. But once he met her, he thought she was intelligent and spirited.

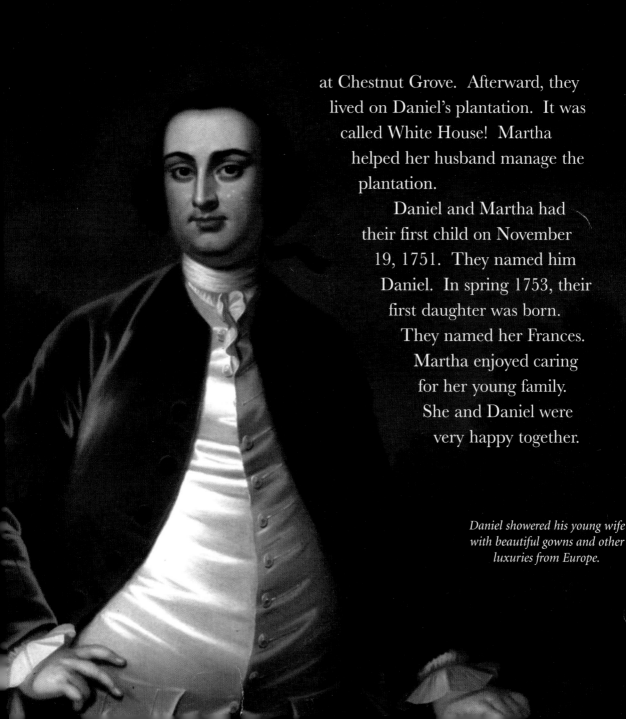

at Chestnut Grove. Afterward, they
lived on Daniel's plantation. It was
called White House! Martha
helped her husband manage the
plantation.

Daniel and Martha had
their first child on November
19, 1751. They named him
Daniel. In spring 1753, their
first daughter was born.
They named her Frances.
Martha enjoyed caring
for her young family.
She and Daniel were
very happy together.

*Daniel showered his young wife
with beautiful gowns and other
luxuries from Europe.*

Early Heartbreak

Unfortunately, Martha's happiness did not last. In February 1754, little Daniel died. Martha and Daniel were very upset. But later that year, their son John was born. They called him Jacky. Then in 1756, their daughter Martha was born. They called her Patsy. It seemed that life would be happy again.

However, Frances died before her fourth birthday in 1757. Children often died during colonial times. Doctors did not have the medicines needed to treat many illnesses. Martha and Daniel felt deep sorrow at the loss of their children.

Just three months later, both Daniel and Jacky became ill. Jacky recovered, but Daniel died in July 1757. Martha was heartbroken when her husband died. She was just 26 years old and had two young children to care for.

After losing her first two children, Martha became overprotective of Jacky and Patsy.

White House sat along the Pamunkey River, just four miles (6 km) from Martha's childhood home.

Martha also needed to manage the plantation. She made sure the shipments of tobacco were ready to be sent to Great Britain. And, she wrote letters to British merchants to arrange fair prices for the tobacco. Some of Daniel's workers helped her. However, Martha knew she could not run things alone for long. She would need to marry again.

A New Beginning

Martha had become one of Virginia's wealthiest widows. Many men wanted to marry her for this reason. But, Martha did not want to marry someone who only wanted her money. She wanted to find a man who would be a good father to Jacky and Patsy.

In spring 1758, Martha was having dinner with friends when a stranger arrived. The stranger was George Washington, an officer in Virginia's army. He wanted to meet Martha, but he did not plan to stay long. Yet when he saw her, he did not want to leave! He liked Martha very much.

Martha felt the same way about George. A few weeks later, he asked her to marry him. George did

By the time Martha met George, he had already become a military hero in Virginia.

not have a lot of money. So, many people thought he wanted to marry Martha because she was wealthy. But Martha knew better. She and George got along well. He liked her children, too.

Martha told George she would like to marry him. So, they were wed at White House on January 6, 1759. Martha was 27 years old and ready to begin a new life.

George and Martha's wedding was a festive occasion for family and friends. The couple celebrated for several days with Jacky, Patsy, and their many guests.

Life at Mount Vernon

Mrs. Washington and her children moved to Mount Vernon, their new home in Virginia. They loved the house right away. And, Mr. Washington left the army to be near his new family.

The **newlyweds** were very busy. Mr. Washington managed the plantation while Mrs. Washington cared for the house and the children.

Mr. and Mrs. Washington kept busy by growing a variety of crops. Their farm produced wheat, corn, potatoes, oats, and rye.

And together, they entertained many guests at Mount Vernon.

Mr. Washington was a good stepfather to Jacky and Patsy. He loved them very much. The children were happy at Mount Vernon, but their mother worried. Jacky was not doing well with his schoolwork. And, Patsy was sick with **epilepsy**. Sadly, she died of the disease on June 19, 1773.

Mrs. Washington was not sure she could bear another tragedy. Yet, being at Mount Vernon with her husband and Jacky made her happy again. The Washingtons were content to lead their lives in Virginia. But fate had a different plan.

Mount Vernon was a beautiful plantation. The Washingtons enjoyed a dramatic view of the Potomac River from their front porch.

A Helping Hand

In February 1774, Jacky married a young woman named Nelly Calvert. Meanwhile, tensions were growing between the North

Many of the soldiers at Valley Forge, Pennsylvania, were catching harmful diseases. Still, Mrs. Washington wanted to be with her husband.

American colonists and Great Britain. The colonists were angry because Great Britain wanted them to pay high taxes. Soon, news of the **Boston Tea Party** reached the Washingtons.

Some colonists held a meeting and formed a group called the **Continental Congress**. Mr. Washington attended the meeting in Philadelphia, Pennsylvania. The colonies planned to go to war against Great Britain to gain their independence. In 1775, the Continental Congress asked Mr. Washington to be the Continental army's general.

During the **American Revolution**, General Washington could not stay at Mount Vernon. So, Mrs. Washington spent each winter with him in the army camps. The cold months were difficult. Many of the soldiers did not have food, warm clothes, or even shoes. Mrs. Washington wanted to help. So, she knit socks and shirts for them. The soldiers gratefully called her "Lady Washington."

Women of the Revolution

Before the American Revolution began, Great Britain's King George III passed several acts. These laws limited the rights of American colonists and their way of life. This angered the colonists. But, they worked to show the king that they would not submit to his unfair rules. Colonial women found ways to make homemade clothes, paper, and other materials. This way, they would not have to depend on Britain for anything.

Women played an important role during the war. Some women made uniforms, shirts, and socks for the soldiers. Others collected scrap metal to make bullets. Many women learned to manage their farms and stores while their husbands served as soldiers. And near the battlefield, women were often found cooking, washing, and sewing. Some women even disguised themselves as men so they could fight!

Mrs. Washington's role in the Revolution was also meaningful. Mr. Washington served as commander in chief of the Continental army. His soldiers were hungry, injured, and sick. But, Mrs. Washington kept his spirits up. She also urged the wives of other officers to knit socks for the soldiers. The socks protected the soldiers' feet from getting cold or wet while they marched. Today, Mrs. Washington is remembered for her patriotic efforts during the Revolution.

The wives of other officers set aside their fancy embroidery when they found Mrs. Washington knitting wool socks.

A New Nation

In 1781, Jacky joined the army. Soon after, Mrs. Washington received terrible news that he was sick. Within a few days, Jacky died. Mrs. Washington was very sad. She knew his wife, Nelly, would need help. So, Mrs. Washington adopted two of her grandchildren.

The **American Revolution** continued until 1783. Afterward, General Washington returned to Mount Vernon. He was ready for a quiet life with his family. But, he did not stay home for long.

The British troops surrendered to General Washington on October 19, 1781, after the Battle of Yorktown, in Virginia.

The colonies were now one independent nation. They called their country the United States of America. And New York City, New York, was named the nation's capital. In 1789, the U.S. **Constitution** was signed. Now, the United States needed a strong leader. Everyone agreed that General Washington should be the first president.

At first, the general did not want to lead the country. But, Mrs. Washington knew the nation needed him. General Washington eventually accepted the nomination that forever changed their lives.

Mrs. Washington was relieved when the war ended. And, she was grateful her family was together again.

First Lady

In 1789, General Washington went to New York City to be sworn in as president. Mrs. Washington joined him a few days later. She was surprised by how many people wanted to see her. Crowds lined the streets. They cheered and waved as her carriage drove past.

Mrs. Washington's new duties kept her busy. As First Lady, she helped the president arrange meetings with government officials. She also ran the house they were staying in and held parties and dinners for the citizens of New York. The Washingtons met many interesting people during their years there.

Mr. Washington's inauguration took place at Federal Hall in New York City on April 30, 1789.

However, the First Lady did not enjoy being so busy. She missed her life at Mount Vernon. In a letter to her niece, she wrote, "I have not had one half hour to myself since the day of my arrival." Still, Mrs. Washington worked hard. She knew President Washington and the United States needed her to be strong.

Mrs. Washington hosted many receptions. There, Americans could discuss their ideas with the president and First Lady.

Setting an Example

The United States had never before had a First Lady. So, Mrs. Washington determined what her duties should be. She wanted to set a good example for the American people. The First Lady never asked for special treatment. And, she always treated others fairly. Mrs. Washington's attitude made her a popular hostess.

President Washington was a serious leader. But, Mrs. Washington's friendly manner put him at ease with their guests.

Mrs. Washington also made time for family. Her adopted grandchildren, Nelly and Wash, loved New York City. They enjoyed outings to museums and theaters. And every Saturday, the family took a carriage ride through the city.

On July 4, 1790, the president and First Lady hosted a large Independence Day celebration. Cannons and drums welcomed their guests. The Washingtons served cake to hundreds of people. Everyone was happy to celebrate the country's independence.

Later that year, the nation's capital moved to Philadelphia, Pennsylvania. This meant the president and First Lady needed to move, too. Crowds of people gathered to say good-bye. A 13-gun salute marked their farewell. In Philadelphia, the Washingtons continued to host parties for important guests. Mrs. Washington enjoyed her time there.

Americans continue to gather each year on July 4 to watch local fireworks displays.

Second Term

President Washington's first term ended in 1793. He wanted to go home to Mount Vernon. But, the United States still faced many challenges. Everyone said President Washington was the only person who could keep the nation together.

In March 1793, President Washington began his second term. Many problems arose for him to solve. He worked to improve relations between Native Americans and colonists. And, he worked to resolve conflicts with Great Britain, France, and other countries.

Meanwhile, government officials argued about how to run the country. The president was popular, but he could not keep everyone happy. Through these troubled times, Mrs. Washington did her best to support her

Mrs. Washington was very protective of the president. She became angry whenever he was criticized.

Today, visitors can tour the beautifully restored Mount Vernon. The home is located just 16 miles (26 km) south of Washington, D.C., on the Potomac River.

husband. In 1797, President Washington finished his second term. This time, he said he would not be president again.

John Adams became the second president of the United States. So, the Washingtons were finally able to return to Mount Vernon. The former president was happy to be a farmer again. His hard work made their home beautiful. And, Mrs. Washington was relieved to be with her family once more.

Last Years

In 1799, Mrs. Washington's granddaughter Nelly married Mr. Washington's nephew Lawrence Lewis. Mrs. Washington was overjoyed when the couple had a baby girl that November. She loved spending time with her growing family.

Unfortunately, Mr. Washington soon caught a terrible cold. He died on December 14, 1799. Mrs. Washington missed her husband very much. So, she kept busy by taking care of the house and her family. On May 22, 1802, she died at home of old age. She was buried next to Mr. Washington at Mount Vernon.

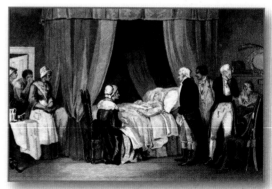

After her husband died, Mrs. Washington refused to live in the rooms they had shared. Instead, she spent the rest of her days in the attic.

Mrs. Washington had a challenging job as America's original First Lady. It was not the life she had hoped for. But, she knew her husband needed her to do her best. The United States needed her, too. Martha Washington met the challenge with courage. She set a fine example as the first of America's First Ladies.

Mrs. Washington will always be honored for her strength during the founding of a nation.

Timeline

1731	Martha Dandridge was born on June 2.
1750	Martha married Daniel Parke Custis on May 15.
1751	Martha and Daniel's son Daniel was born.
1753	Martha and Daniel's daughter Frances was born.
1754	Martha and Daniel's son Daniel died; their son John, or Jacky, was born.
1756	Martha and Daniel's daughter Martha, or Patsy, was born.
1757	Frances died; Martha's husband Daniel died.
1759	Martha married George Washington on January 6.
1773	Patsy died of epilepsy.
1775	Mr. Washington began leading the Continental army.
1781	Jacky died shortly after joining the army; the Washingtons adopted two of their grandchildren.
1789–1797	Mrs. Washington acted as First Lady, while her husband served as president.
1790	The Washingtons relocated when the capital moved from New York City, New York, to Philadelphia, Pennsylvania.
1799	Mr. Washington died on December 14.
1802	Mrs. Washington died on May 22.

Did You Know?

Mrs. Washington loved having company. In fact, between 1768 and 1775, the Washingtons hosted more than 2,000 guests in their home!

In addition to running Mount Vernon's farms, Mrs. Washington also oversaw cloth-making. The plantation produced enough material to clothe 316 workers.

In 1776, the Continental navy named the USS *Lady Washington* after Mrs. Washington. It is the first U.S. military ship to be named in honor of a woman or a First Lady.

While she was First Lady, Mrs. Washington owned a pet parrot.

Mrs. Washington was the first president's widow to receive a gift from Congress. She was granted free postage to reply to the thousands of sympathy letters she received after her husband died.

Mrs. Washington's privacy was important to her. So, she burned almost every letter she and President Washington ever exchanged.

In 1902, the first U.S. stamp honoring a woman was released. It featured Martha Washington and cost eight cents.

Glossary

American Revolution - from 1775 to 1783. A war for independence between Great Britain and its North American colonies. The colonists won and created the United States of America.

Boston Tea Party - December 16, 1773. About 60 Boston colonists, dressed as Native Americans, boarded a ship in Boston Harbor. They threw a shipment of tea overboard to protest the Stamp Act of 1765.

Constitution - the laws that govern the United States.

Continental Congress - the body of representatives that spoke for and acted on behalf of the 13 colonies.

epilepsy - a disorder involving repeated seizures. Seizures are episodes of disturbed brain function that cause changes in attention and behavior.

newlywed - a person who just married.

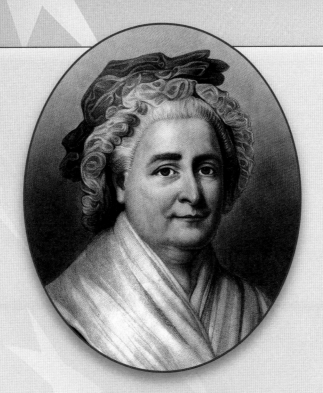

Web Sites

To learn more about Martha Washington, visit ABDO Publishing Company on the World Wide Web at **www.abdopublishing.com**. Web sites about Martha Washington are featured on our Book Links page. These links are routinely monitored and updated to provide the most current information available.

Index